MOTOR SPORTS

Vroom! Vroom! Vroom!

Motor sports are a group of competitive events that mainly involve the use of motor vehicles like cars, bikes and trucks. Motor sports can be broadly classified into racing and non-racing events. They are extreme sports or adventure sports.

Motor sports are extremely popular. The rising popularity of these sports coincides with the growing popularity of television. Motor sports first started out as televised events. Even to this day, several shows are dedicated to these sports.

Different types of vehicles are used for motor sports. Some of these are stock cars which are customised just for the purpose of a motor-racing event. Some are designed and built from scratch, keeping these events in mind. Cars used in drag racing and rally racing are examples of the latter. Formula one racing cars are custom-built for the races. Even lawnmowers are used in motor sports. Motor sports occupy a specific niche in the society and are often depicted in various movies, books and other media. Motor sports also make for popular computer games.

Did You Know? The jargon used in motor sports have made their way into several languages. "Burning rubber" is a phrase which means "to drive very fast". Similarly, "need for speed" (which is also a popular computer game) is used to urge someone to drive faster.

Auto Racing

Auto racing is a very popular motor sport. Even non-enthusiasts follow these races. It is a race in which the drivers need to reach the finish line in the least possible time.

Origin

Auto racing as a sport developed shortly after the invention of fuel cars. This sport gained popularity because of the sheer human nature of competition.

The first auto racing competition was to be held in the city of Paris in 1887. The track was only 2-km long. Only one contestant showed up, so it was abandoned. But by 1894, the sport was actually taken up in a good form and held over a distance of 127 km.

Soon, there were more races held with people participating from several countries. This was a mark of the growing popularity and globalisation of the sport. Very soon, purposeful race tracks were built to conduct these races.

Gameplay

The most famous types of races are:

- **Formula Racing:** This is the most popular form of auto racing. It is a single-seated racing, as only individual participants race against each other. Cars are custom-built for these races. One of the unique features is that the wheels have no covers unlike normal cars. These cars have special wings attached, which allow the driver to easily manoeuvre the car on the race track. The international format of racing is called "Formula One Racing".

Protective head gear is a must in all Formula Racing events. Many dangerous injuries have been reported in the past.

- **Touring car racing:** This race uses road-going cars which you might see on your way to work or school. However, these cars are heavily modified to suit the race track. These cars are heavy and offer less speed than Formula Racing cars. This type of racing is called "full contact race driving". Players prefer garage-made race cars to compete in this sport. This means that the cars are modified to suit their preferences.
- **Sports car racing:** This is a closed-circuit race. It uses sports cars that are custom-built or modified to suit the race track. They are closed cockpit cars with covered wheels, aiming at raw speed and endurance-based performance.

Formula Racing is also called "single-seated car racing" because only one driver is involved.

- **Production car racing:** This is also called "showroom stock racing" in the USA. It is heavily restricted by rules.
- **One-make car racing:** All the cars in these races are produced by one manufacturer. If only one model of a car is raced, then that also falls into this category. They have limited rules and are mainly conducted as promotional events.
- **Stock car racing:** After Formula Racing, this is the second-most popular form of racing. It is run on oval-shaped tracks. The players must complete a certain number of laps in the least amount of time. NASCAR is the most popular example of this type.
- **Rallying:** Cars compete on public roads or rough terrains which are closed for the race. All participants have a "co-driver" who tries to attain certain points. The race is done in stages and uses road-legal production-based cars.

The cars are chosen based on the type of road or terrain on which the race will be held. If the terrain is extremely rough and dusty, the car will be bigger and stronger.

Rules

Each type of auto racing has its own set of rules. NASCAR issues a different rule book for each of its series. Their rules are not shared with the public and can only be accessed by NASCAR racers.

In Formula Racing, the drivers are allotted points according to the position at which they have finished the race. For example, the first place has 10 points while the last place has 1 point.

In Stock Car Racing, it is a well-known rule that all participating cars must be of the same level. The engine is the only exception.

Wall of fame

Giedo van der Garde is a Dutch racing driver.

Tony Stewart is a stock car racing 2005 Infineon champion.

Andreas Mikkelsen is a VW Polo R WRC racing pro.

Fact card

- The first auto race that took place had only one participant, and he declared himself as the winner.
- The stock cars can reach up to 322 kmph.
- Early races used to be held on streets and beaches to increase their popularity.
- Any driver who fails to complete an auto race, no matter what the reason, is considered to be "retired" or "out".
- The positions of the retired drivers are determined by the order in which they have retired.

Motorcycle Racing

Motorbike racing, as a sport, is dangerous and exciting. It is fun to observe the bikes going on and off the road. The sport focusses on skills, stunts or sometimes both. Motorbike racing is a highly dangerous and thrilling sport. The rules of safety and protection are not as developed as they are in car racing.

Origin

Motorcycle racing gained popularity in 1904, when the Federation of International Motorcycling was formed.

Once the sport gained fame, people from all the major countries showed interest in participating in the competitions. There were certain arguments about the racing conditions, which caused slight problems within the committees. By 1936, a better committee was established. The rules and priorities of the committees were agreed upon by all. With this, more and more countries began to participate.

Motorcycle races are conducted in rough terrains where the bikers must go down a hill.

In 1998, the committee was formed with the basis of permanent fixed rules for various genres of motorcycle racing. This is the world of motorcycle racing that we are all familiar with today. Motorcycle racing is also called "moto racing" or "bike racing". Motorcycle racing can be broadly classified into two categories: road racing and off-road racing. There are also sub categories like circuit racing, open course racing, track racing, drag racing and hill climbs.

All motorcycle racers wear helmets as a precaution against head injuries.

All participants wear special gloves to tightly grip the handles of the motorbikes.

Motorcycle racers wear bodysuits to protect their bodies from injuries during a fall.

The feet and knees of the racers are heavily protected to avoid friction when they come in contact with the road.

Types of racing

There are various forms of racing based on the type of motorbike, as well as terrain.

Road racing: These races are held on open roads which are blocked from public use. These roads are tested for racing beforehand.

Motorcycle grand prix: This is the most famous type of motorbike racing. It has three distinct classes in itself.

Moto3 uses 250 CC bikes. These races have an age barrier of 25 years but wild card entries can be as old as 28 years.

Moto2 uses 600 CC four-stroke bikes.

Moto GP is the highest class of GP racing where 990 CC four-stroke engine bikes are allowed.

In traditional road racing, there are two championships which exist to this day. They are International Road Racing Championship and Duke Road Racing Championship. There is also a Duke Road Racing Rankings List.

Superbike racing: These races use modified production bikes. The criteria is to have four-stroke engines in the 750 CC to 1200 CC range. Supersport racing checks the endurance of the equipment rather than the skill of the biker.

Sidecar racing and traditional bike racing are some examples of this type of racing.

Motocross: It is a direct equivalent of road racing. However, it is done off the road and on rough terrains. The terrains can be covered with dirt, sand, mud or grass. Here, the skill of the biker is tested as they have to pull off jumps and other such stunts on their bikes. The usual criteria is to finish a set number of laps in the least amount of time. However, the criteria might change per race.

Supercross, Supermoto and cross country biking are other forms of off-road bike racing.

Wall of fame

Stefan William Merriman was born in New Zealand. He is a contender for the World Enduro Championship. He has participated from the Husqvarna and Yamaha teams. He has also represented Honda. He has won the championship four times.

Marco Simoncelli was an Italian motorcycle racer who competed in the Road Racing World Championship for 10 years from 2002 to 2011. In 2008, he won the 250 CC World Championship Race.

Fact card

- The front tyre provides more than 75 per cent of the grip during a steep turn.
- The first bike ever made was an 1869 steam cycle.
- Devil, Satan and Lucifer are names of some brands of motorcycle. These names are a result of it popularly being called a "devil sport".
- Valentine Rossi started riding bikes at a very tender age. His passion for racing began with kart racing.
- Road racing is done on tarmac roads. It is also conducted in purpose-built racing circuits.

Motor Rallying

Motor rallying is an off-road racing event. Drivers and navigators form a team that moves from Point A to Point B in the shortest possible time over a variety of terrains. The terrains are usually rough and dusty.

This is a production car which has been modified and updated to run on dusty, dirt terrains.

Origin

The word "rally" dates back to 1911, when city-to-city races used to happen. Rallies usually consisted of roads that were not as well built as they are today. Therefore, this sport became famous for its different nature and rough touch.

Soon races began, and the exposure to elements being high, the cars were modified accordingly. The usual average speed, which was 24 kmph, now advanced to over 105 kmph. To make this even more exciting, some countries made huge indoor patches to host these races. They put in artificial terrain conditions. This garned more attention.

However, during World War I, the popularity of the game saw a decline. Much later, the commercial car companies got into the production of rally cars, and soon enough, the game started taking off again. Today, the world rally competition has participants contesting from all the continents.

Unlike other types of rally races, motor rallies are won by completing the track in the least amount of time. This is similar to other races, however, the point-to-point system of rally races also applies here.

Rally races also follow some formats of auto racing.

The production of the cars, like in auto racing, is done keeping the races in mind.

The wheels of the rally cars are specially modified to endure rough terrains.

Rules

- The objective of the rally races is to complete the race in the least possible time. But it also has stage settings and the drivers can change places stage wise. This increases the complexity of the game.
- The cars used for this sport are modified off-road vehicles. Vehicles need to be checked completely before they can legally become rally vehicles.
- There are two main forms of rallying. These are stage rallies and road rallies. Stage rallies have a professional approach to the game. Participants have to go through various terrains in order to test the car in all conditions for overall endurance.

The most popular form of a road rally is the one that takes place on a highway. The highways are kept blocked for the public. The emphasis of the road rallies that take place on highways shifts from being speed focused to control and navigation focused. The races need to be completed in the least amount of time. The earlier forms of rallies were called "trails". Rallying is considered as the grass root for motor racing development.

There are other types of rallies that take place on all kinds of terrains. These can be made of asphalt, mud, ice, snow or even gravel. A typical rally race has a set time limit. If not completed within the stipulated time the racer would be disqualified.

Britain, France, Scandinavia and Belgium are the most important countries of rally racing. It is also popular in the USA. Each of these countries have adapted to the changes that have taken place in the rally racing world. The most important and popular drivers of rally racing hail from these countries. However, before the 1950s, the racers were amateur drivers who were paid next to nothing for racing.

Notice that the driver of this car is going through a dirty road. He must wear a helmet which protects his head and eyes.

It was in the 1960s that the world of rally racing got its first superstar. His name was Erik Carlsson and he hailed from Sweden. He drove a Saab. He inspired people around the world to take part in rally racing. At the time, the spread of rally racing was limited to the European region. Now, it is present in all continents of the world. The World Rally Championship accepts people from all countries.

Wall of fame

Erik Carlsson was nicknamed as Mr Saab because of the PR he had done for the company. He became famous for the unusual steps he took during his career. He was also known for his innovative rallying tactics.

Sebastien Loeb is considered as one of the greatest rally drivers of all time. Born in France, he began rally driving in 1995 and has competed in several races. He has won eight World Rally Championship (WRC) titles.

Fact card

- This form of racing was developed after a city run on a car that did not take the proper route.
- The race was considered an entertainer for the terrain changes and the limited stunts that it offered.
- Initially, none of the drivers were paid. They were only reimbursed for the expenses they bore.
- The rallies follow a process called "reconnaissance" or "recce" in which the co-driver writes down shorthand notes on how to drive a stage.

Snowmobile Racing

A snowmobile is a vehicle which is specially designed for travelling in the snow. Snowmobile racing involves traversing a set course in these vehicles. It originated as a fairly non-competitive sport and even today, most courses are natural.

Origin

Earlier, snowmobiles were built to travel on snow and ice. They had no cover, except a small windshield, and also consisted of rubber tracks. They were designed to travel on snow and did not need a carved path for it. They had a gasoline two stroke engine.

These machines were built for hunters and working officials to use during winter, to make their passage easier and more efficient. Later, they were used for recreational purposes.

The riders were known as snowmobile riders. This took the form of racing as we see it today.

Snowmobiles are also used in snowy regions as a transport vehicle.

There are different types of snowmobiles. Some are only suitable for less snow coverage.

Rules

The game is inclined for fun and falls under the category of X-games. This is because it is an extreme adventure sport. Safety is the most important concern of this game, and also the vehicle type used.

Snowmobiles have to have a validation check to fit the criteria required for the competition. There are various forms of racing and therefore rules differ, but these baseline rules are the same for any kind of race. Asphalt, cross country, drag, enduro, hill climb, ice lemans, oval sprint, snow cross and sprint running are a few common types of races. They follow the generalised rules of other motor sports in addition to the basics mentioned above. Youth crossing and water cross competition are also very famous.

Fact card

- The economic impact of snowmobiling in the USA is more than 26 billion US dollars annually.
- The average use of a snowmobile in North America is about 1891 km per year.

Truck Racing

Trucks are generally heavy vehicles that are used to carry freight and built for tonnage rather than speed. However, from truckers' friendly competition evolved the sport of truck racing. Today, it is mostly contested on outdoor tracks with specially modified vehicles.

There are many types of trucks. There are some pick-up trucks which are also used for racing.

Origin

The sport came into notice in June, 1979. An association was formed, which held the truck races, and it was a spectator sport where no specialised trucks were present.

The general fare, normal production trucks with the least amount of modification were used in the earlier races. The trucks ran on oval circuits on lap-based races, or on single long-distance tracks. But, they started hitting speeds of 130 kmph, and that's when the need for specialisation arose. In order to win the races, some drivers forgo safety. The specialised trucks were an answer to the problem of safety. In order to gain more speed, the trucks were made lighter.

Considering the safety angle, certain changes were made in the regulations. Finally, the sport that we play today is completely monitored in terms of safety and danger.

Rules

The first concern of a large vehicle is safety. Therefore, there are basic rules set for it. Racers cannot cross the speed limit of 160 kmph. The minimum weight limit of the racing trucks is 5500 kg.

On a professional level, the racers have to compete in races that have 8–10 laps. There is only slight contact between trucks during the game, otherwise it is a non-contact race.

Minimum contact is maintained in order to minimise driver injuries and vehicle destruction.

The leading truck races are now controlled by the Motor Sports Association and the world championship has over 30 teams competing regularly for the same.

All trucks are modified to endure any terrain. Drivers wear protective clothes and helmets.

Like in the other races, truck racing is done in any terrain and weather. The trucks are strong and built for all climates.

Fact card

- In certain races, the engines of the trucks run on alcohol.
- Racers need a published motor sport association license along with a normal driving license to compete in these races.

Hovercraft Racing

Hovercrafts are vehicles that appear to be moving on thin air. They ride along on a cushion of air and can traverse a variety of rough terrain.

Origin

Hovercraft is also known as an air cushion vehicle. The idea for the hovercraft was born in 1716. At the time, it was called "the fast torpedo boat". It could move at the speed of 32 knots or 59 kmph. Hovercrafts later came to be used in wars as armoured vehicles.

After the war, the hoverboard came to be used for recreational activities. Soon, this recreational activity turned into a sport. Hovercraft clubs were formed. There are several hovercraft competitions held in a year.

Hovercraft racing is done on water. Hoverboards are a fairly new invention.

Gameplay

The sport is a one-day event, where all precautions are taken and buoys or markers are set to show the guiding path to the start and finish line.

The prime focus is safety. There is a checklist to the race event and at a given time, only a specific number of participants are allowed to take off. It can be held over land, as well as water.

Depending on the institution, they decide the race surface and criteria. There can be cruising sessions as well. The regulations change as per event, but the baseline remains the same.

The wheel at the back of the hovercraft gives speed to the vehicle.

The bottom of the hovercraft can bump and move over every type of terrain.

Hovercraft racing uses specially designed hovercrafts. Smaller hovercrafts are for personal use. There are only a handful of hovercraft races held on land.

Hovercrafts created for leisure can carry up to four people at one time. They are built for land and for water. They can even pass swamps and icy lands. However, not all hovercrafts can do this. Some hovercrafts are built as yacht tenders. They can transport people travelling in one yacht to another.

Some hovercrafts are even used in place of jet-skis. In remote areas surrounded by water, hovercrafts are used as a mode of transporting goods from one place to another. These are called "hoverbarges" and can carry nearly 250 tonnes of goods. Hoverbarges move slower and are bigger in size, so they cannot be used for racing and are made of aircraft technology.

Fact card

- The hovercraft floats slightly over air and can move on any surface.
- The biggest hovercraft can carry 418 passengers.

Lawnmower Racing

We cannot be sure who looked at a lawnmower and thought that it would make a wonderful racing vehicle. But we do know that it has become a popular sport amongst the younger generations. Today, it is a fairly popular mainstream sport.

Origin

The sport was founded in the UK in 1973. It is said to have been invented by young racing enthusiasts who could not afford any other kind of motor sport. This led to the formation of a lawnmower foundation group. This group held several competitions to fellow racing enthusiasts.

However, another story claims that this sport began in the USA in 1963. Factory workers had created the sport as a recreational activity. Nonetheless, it is practiced in many parts of the world today and enjoyed as a sport.

Protective helmets are a must in lawnmower racing.

In some cases, the lawnmowers are custom-built for the races.

Racers compete on one wide track.

- The qualification speed is around 30-48 kmph.
- Only 33 participants are allowed to start at one time.
- There is a back team which has a two-person pit crew and a lap judge.

The rules are different for different age groups, despite being most popular in the younger age groups.

There are different classes ranging from A to D as per competitions.

Rules

There are basic rules set for any variation in this sport:

- Firstly, the blades are removed from the mover for safety purposes.
- The engines are retained, and capacity is kept into consideration prior to competition composition.
- The standard competitions have a lap system. They compete for 60 laps in a 1 or 2 km area.

As seen in all other races, in lawnmower races, the participants wear helmets and protective bodysuits.

Fact card

- In the USA, nearly 85 million households have their own lawnmowers.

All-Terrain Vehicle Racing

All-terrain vehicles (ATVs), as the name suggests, can be driven on all types of terrains. These vehicles have large wheels. They are sturdy. They are also called "quadricycles". Today, ATV racing involves either time-based or endurance-based races.

Origin

In 1893, Royal Enfield built the first quadricycle. It mimicked the modern day ATV. These vehicles were originally built for the military who needed to move through any kind of terrain in any condition.

A commercial company then started building these for recreational purposes. Later on, they were fitted with disc brakes. Thus, ATV racing then became a sport. Within three years, the vehicles were enhanced with four-stroke engines and had a capacity of 190 CC and 38 horsepower racing. Today leading companies have taken over the production, and high powered ATVs are used for racing.

Like car and motor racing, ATV is a highly televised event.

Rules

Safety has always been a concern in ATV racing due to the number of injuries seen in the past. Helmets, padding, protective body suit and other such safety wear are essential for the competition. Without these, the players are not allowed to take part in the race. Players wear protective eye gear, chest protectors, as well as vehicle modifications to keep them firm. In competitions, it is used in hill races, desert races, ice races and dirt races.

ATV racing is an extreme adventure sport.

Fact card

ATVs are also called "quad bikes". Recently, ATV bikes were created by a German company. These bikes combined the features of a motorbike and a quad bike.

ATV races have sprint and endurance categories. They are used in drag races and rallies. ATV racing is done for two categories: amateur racers and pro racers.

As per the age group and vehicle qualification, they are placed in order of races. They are further divided into three-wheeler and four-wheeler racing sections.

Bearing the ability to race on any terrain, this kind of racing covers all sorts of terrains, with all possible genres.

AIR SPORTS

The equipment used in air sports is such that it moves faster when in the air. These sports take place in the sky. Most of these involve the use of some sort of equipment, to control one's fall or glide. Air sports are considered exhilarating. Most air sports are thought of as daredevil sports.

Due to the safety concerns and the necessity of either a plane or a proper location, air sports often tend to require thorough preparation and forethought.

As one can imagine, air sports tend to involve a larger element of risk than any other sport. The participant is often at the mercy of wind and gravity. When they were newly invented, injuries, accidents and deaths were reported on a fairly regular basis. Today, with the improvements made in technology, equipment and safety precautions, air sports have become very safe.

Did you know? A hot air balloon ride is not possible during the monsoon. This is because the heat from the balloon can cause the water around it to boil. Boiling water can destroy the fabric of the balloon.

Banzai Skydiving

Banzai skydiving is a very popular variation of the original form of sky diving. It is considered to be a very dangerous sport as there are a lot of things left to chance.

Origin

This game originated in Japan. It has always been considered a very dangerous sport. It is famously known as "a socially acceptable attempt to suicide".

Banzai skydiving is a very popular sport. There are many televised instances of people attempting banzai skydiving. The shows are also very popular. But this sport caused several near-fatal accidents. Still, nearly two million divers enrol for it every year.

Gameplay

The game is based on the concept of terminal velocity. The parachute is dropped before the player takes the jump. This is dangerous because the diver might not be able to control the parachute's weight.

During a successful dive, the diver catches hold of the parachute and glides to the projected landing zone.

The dive is taken from a height of 10,000 feet. A small cord connects the diver and the parachute. This helps the diver trace the parachute in the air and catch hold of it.

There is a short training session for all participants. During this time, a certified trainer rides with the learner.

Fact card

- Though banzai skydiving is known to have caused several near-fatal accidents, there have been no recorded reports of death due to this sport.

Some people tend to go Banzai skydiving with their partners, friends or family relatives. But a lot of training is required to do this.

The ideal waiting time before making the jump for the parachute is two seconds. In some cases, the wait can be as long as 10 seconds. This is extremely dangerous. Yasuhiro Kubo took a 50 second break before jumping for the chute. This is a Guinness World Record.

Even though the Guinness Book of World Records accepts banzai skydiving records, it does not accept records that were made by taking huge risks. This is because other people might attempt to break it. They also check to make sure that all the guidelines are followed. Some even risk skydiving without a parachute. Very few of these records have been accepted into the Guinness Book of World Records.

This sport cannot be performed in public places. This is for the safety of the diver, as well as the people in public places.

The cord connecting the diver and the parachute ensures that the diver can safely recover his/her parachute. The regular harness required a thread connection which is impossible to handle in the freefall style of the Banzai dive.

Hot Air Ballooning

Hot air ballooning is a sport which evolved from friendly competition. It involves the use of large hot air balloons. The objective is to either travel the highest or the farthest from the starting point.

Origin

Aerostat Reveillon was the first hot air balloon that took off in 1783. Its passengers were a sheep, a duck and a rooster. The balloon was up for under 10 minutes. The first hot air balloon with a human was tethered to the ground. It took off just two months after the first one. It stayed in the air for more than 20 minutes. In the next two years, the activity became so famous that people were flying over the English Channel in hot air balloons.

In 1935, a milestone was set when a hot air balloon rose more than 22-km high in the air. In 1999, the first record for travelling around the world in a hot air balloon was set. Hot air ballooning has become a recreational sport, but has also retained its competitive angle.

Types of hot air ballooning

There are two types of records that can be made; vertical distance travelled and horizontal distance travelled. Often called as "races", hot air ballooning competitions are mostly about accuracy and not speed.

In one of the forms, the goal of the pilot is to fly as close as possible to pre-decided points called "targets". The pilot must know about the different wind directions at different altitudes. He/she is given topographic maps and GPS units beforehand, which help determine the navigation route to take for the race.

Another form of competition is the "hare and hound". In this, the hare balloons take off before the hound balloons, which eventually chase the former.

Over 750 hot air balloons participate in the annual hot air balloon festival in Albuquerque, New Mexico.

The balloons are made of nomex and nylon.

The burner gasifies liquid propane.

The basket is made of light material and carries the passengers.

Fact card

- Captain Joseph Kittinger made a world record by jumping out of a hot air balloon and breaking the sound barrier with the speed of his falling body.
- Jean-François Pilatre De Rozier lost his life during his journey across the English Channel. He was the world's first balloonist.

Air Racing

Air racing is a motorsport that involves the use of aircraft to compete over a fixed aerial course at the fastest speed possible. The sport received an impetus from the World Wars and is now fairly popular.

Origin

Air racing came into existence as early as 1909 in France, near Paris. It had different types of major race events, which attracted builders, pilots and architects from around the globe.

The competitions held in the area encouraged people to bring out their best. In no time, better technology and designs were developed. The Gordon Bennett race series was the major development made in this sport. After World War I, there was a sudden pickup in the race scenario, as more and more well-trained pilots started pouring in.

Soon, National Championship Air Races were started. Till date, they take place every year with a booming response.

Those aircraft which allow two seated pilots are called "two-seater aircraft". Most two-seaters are used to train learning pilots. The trainer sits at the back with the learner in the front. Both have control of the craft.

Turboprops are the most common types of aircraft used in air racing. These aircraft use turbine engines. They drive an aircraft propeller. Most of the engine's power is utilised in providing energy to the propeller, which thrusts the aircraft forward.

Rules

There are certain basic rules which are followed in air racing to provide safety. Various flying sessions take place for the selection procedure.

- **Training:** More than two days of sessions by master class pilots are conducted in order to ensure appropriate training over mandatory sessions. The final session of the training period takes the pilots to the next qualifying stage.
- **Qualifiers:** It takes place before the day of the race. If the pilots give their best time, they qualify for the next level.
- **Top 12:** It takes place on the day of the race. Among the top 12 players, there are six winners. Of the remaining six, two are chosen to form the top eight based on their time.

Pilots are also judged on the amount of smoke they release from the aircraft. If there is not enough smoke, or too much smoke is released, the pilot gets disqualified.

Just from the appearance, one can tell that this aircraft is not as heavy as an aeroplane. It seats just two people. Usually, a competition can have one or two pilots. If there are two, it is considered to be a team racing sport.

This model is similar to the Beechcraft T-6 Texan II, which is a single turboprop aircraft. Most aircraft are built by taking inspiration from other aircraft. Even the Beechcraft is built from the Pilatus PC-9.

The pilot needs to radio in during take-off and landing.

The paints of all aircraft are chosen keeping in mind certain rules and regulations. Military aircraft are mostly painted in the flag colours of the countries they hail from.

- **Super eight:** The selected eight players take one flight individually to earn their ranking. The fastest four are selected. The remaining four are ranked as per their speed to decide the positions from the remaining fifth to eighth..
- **Final four:** The fastest player becomes the champion. The rest are given their positions, as per their speeds.

The race track is of either 5 or 6 km. The planes have to go through air gates in order to complete the race. Incorrect orientation or not passing through air gates properly would add to penalty seconds. If extra penalties are considered, then a "did not finish" tag is applied. In certain conditions, disqualification is also possible.

First penalty is based on insufficient or no smoke at all. Second penalty is based on air gate entry and orientation.

The "did not finish" tag is based upon the weight, speed and deviation of the aircraft. Air gates are large polygons, which are used to mark speed.

Wall of fame

Nigel Lamb was the champion of the 2014 racing scene.

Hannes Arch won the 2008 Air Race World Championship.

Paul Bonhomme won the 2015 Red Bull Air Race World Championship. He also won the 2009 and 2010 championships.

Fact card

- Due to World War I, the popularity of the sport reduced. However, as the crafts were used in the war, it produced better pilots.
- There is an additional 10 kg of weight in the tail of the aeroplane to bring its centre of gravity to a better position.
- "The Corvus" is the lightest and most used aeroplane in competitions.
- Formula V Air Racing is one of the most popular air racing competitions in the world today.
- Air racing has taken many forms from pylon races like the Reno Race and Formula One air races to long distance races like the Schneider Trophy.

Paragliding

Paragliding is a sport, which involves the use of a paraglider. It is an unpowered aerial sport and is fairly popular due to its focus on skills rather than strength.

Paragliders must wear protective and strong shoes as during the landing, there is a lot of friction caused on the feet.

Origin

During World War I, parachutes were used by soldiers to get into enemy territories. Then the soldiers would conduct sneak attacks. The navy also used them to tow sailors behind a submarine to observe what they could on the horizon.

In 1950, the Para Commanders were invented. They provided better vent and control of the chute. In 1958, this idea led to the development of gliders. Thus, hang gliders and paragliders were invented.

In 1964, the Ram Air canopy was invented in which the air rammed in, filling the sail; thus forming a wing shape. This was a revolutionary change, which led to the development of the gliders that are used today. Europe has seen the highest number of paragliders.

This man is being trained to ride a paraglider. No one is allowed to paraglide without proper training.

Equipment & Gameplay

Paragliding requires certain essential instruments, such as the wing, harnesses, variometers, radios, as well as GPS units to navigate in the sky. The pilots must be aware of, and know how to use, each and every one of these equipments. Otherwise, they cannot participate in a paragliding activity.

Based on the individual and their level of comfort, there are brakes and methods of manoeuvering the gliders. Weight shift and speed bars are the most important parameters that determine the flight. Big ears, B-line stall and spiral dive are some of the different techniques of flying.

Paraglides are launched into the sky using three main techniques: forward launch, reverse launch and towed launch.

- **Forward launch:** In this technique the pilot runs forward with the wing. This creates a pressure in the air. The wings then get inflated and rise higher. Forward launch is performed closer to the ground where there is low wind.
- **Reverse launch:** This type of launch is best suited for places that experience high winds. The pilot stands facing the wing in order to get it into the flying position. The pilot then runs under the wing to perform the launch. There are several advantages of this type of launch as the pilot can check the lines and also resist the force easily. However, this launch is more complex in comparison to the rest.
- **Towed launch:** The pilot pulls a release cord, and the towline falls away. The towed launch appears less like a take-off and more like a direct flight. The pilot needs special training to execute it. Wings are towed with either a vehicle or a boat.

The upper and diagonal ribs are connected to the lower surface of the paraglider. The cascades are connected to them.

The "strings" of a paraglider are connected to its ribs and diagonal ribs. They are called "cascades".

All paragliders need to wear protective helmets, gloves and padding for safety.

The body is held rigid and the legs are left loose. Any kind of struggle or sudden movement can disturb the flight.

Wall of fame

Nevil Hulett has a straight distance record of 502.9 km.

Robbie Whittall holds a world record for soaring to a height of 4526 m.

Peggy McAlpine is the oldest female paraglider.

- **Traffic pattern:** While landing, one needs to watch out for traffic patterns. Landing involves some amount of planning as several pilots might want to land at the same time in the same area. A traffic pattern lines up the pilots and gives each of them a position above the airfield to the side of the landing area.
- **Soaring:** In this technique, the pilot makes use of the wind to stay at a certain height, or rise higher in the air. To do this, the pilot takes-off from the ridges and uses the hand pedals, and brakes to control the flight.

While flying above a slope, the pilots rely on the air to lift them up. They are forced upwards by the wind. But it is up to the pilot to control the flight. If the pilot cannot control the flight and the movement of the glider, they can put themselves at tremendous risk.

Pilots are safely harnessed to the gliders. The harnesses are checked regularly to ensure that they are safe.

Fact card

- The biggest paragliding wing is 66 feet and can carry a load of around 589 kg.
- Paragliding has been improved to allow people with disabilities to participate in the sport as well.
- The term "paraglider" was coined by NASA.
- When the pilots are at a height of 2 m from the ground, they apply 0 per cent brake. As they touch the ground, they apply 100 per cent brake.
- Before landing, the pilot "flaps" the wing so that it loses its performance and reaches the ground faster.

Hang Gliding

Hang gliding is a common air sport which involves the use of a glider to ride the winds and air currents.

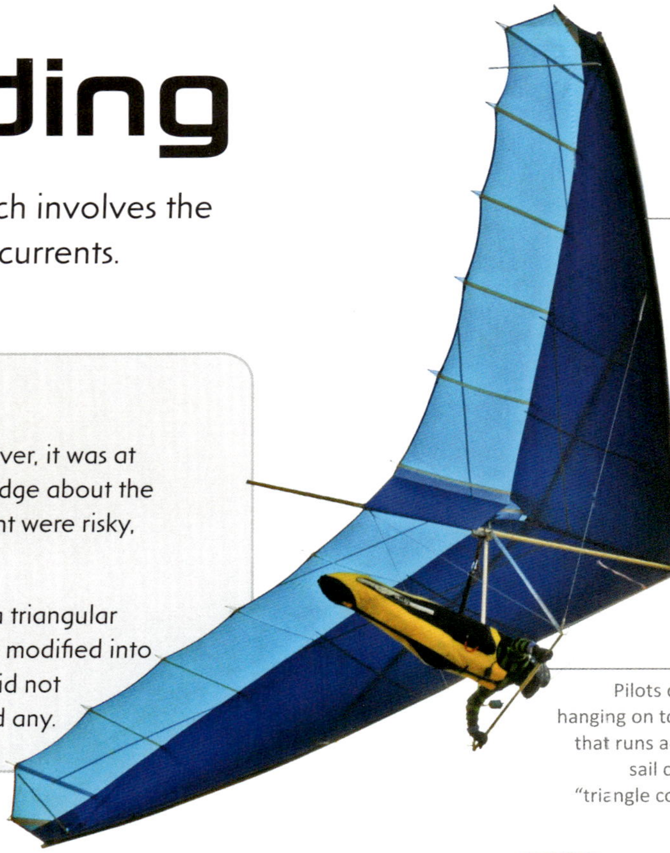

Hang gliders are basically made of sail materials. These are woven polyester fabrics or composite laminated fabrics.

Pilots control the flight by hanging on to the horizontal bar that runs across the triangular sail cloth. It is called the "triangle control frame" (TCF).

Origin

This air sport was invented back in the 1890s. However, it was at a very basic level. People did not have much knowledge about the field of flight dynamics. So, any experiments with flight were risky, as proper safety measures were not in place.

In the year 1904, a flexible wing was built. It had a triangular wireframe which could carry a pilot. Soon, they were modified into hang gliders. Hang gliders had flexible wings. They did not have any other extra equipment as they did not need any.

Rules

The sport has simple rules for landing and take-off. There are a set of rules focussing on flying at a height of 500 m–11,000 feet.

Before a hang glider can take flight, he/she must get the launch site authorised. All pilots must learn how to use the radio, and how to give out call signs before they can hang glide. Only one person should tow the hang glider.

System & competition

The brakes and the direction system are very well defined in this sport. The landing technique is comparatively difficult. A typical take-off is carried out by running and then gaining momentum. Hang gliding competitions take place on the Alps. Hundreds of hang gliders from around the world participate in these competitions. The competitions are based on the accuracy of landing, speed and timing.

Ridge lift, mountain waves, thermal and convergence are the most famous ways of attaining soaring.

All hang gliders have a hang glider sailcloth and triangle control frame.

Fact card

- John W. Dickenson won a gold air medal for his invention of the modern hang glider.
- A group of pilots hang gliding together is called a "gaggle".

BOARD SPORTS

Rare is the child who hasn't seen Tony Hawk and his exploits on a skateboard. Board sports are fairly old, with the invention of the original surfboard being traced back to Polynesia, in 1769.

The primary equipment essential to perform a board sport is any type of board. Many of these board sports have evolved from other sports. They have also evolved from routine methods of transport. The idea for snowboarding came from sleds, which are the vehicles used in snowy regions.

Board sports can be carried out on different types of landforms, from flat surfaces to rough sand deserts. They are played in the snow and on water. All of these sports are conducted outdoors. There are no fixed arenas for these sports. This can often cause damage to property. There is also a certain risk factor involved in this sport. This is the reason they are popular among the younger generations. Many board sports are classified as extreme or adventure sports. Today, the rising popularity of these sports is bringing them to the mainstream.

Did you know? The face, ankles and wrists are most prone to injuries in skateboarding. That is why, it is essential for skateboarders to wear appropriate safety gear.

Skateboarding

Skateboarding is an extremely fun sport. Those who perform this sport are called "skateboarders". This sport is very popular in certain countries. There are skate parks created just for people who indulge in this sport.

Origin

The very first skateboard had wooden boxes with wheels on it. Soon, the wooden boxes were developed into planks which look similar to the contemporary skateboards of today.

The sport itself was born in the 1940s, Bill Richard was the first skateboard producer. At the time, he called it "sidewalk surfing".

Early skateboarders rode the boards barefooted. They would travel along the pathways on their streets. Slowly, the size of the board was reduced and its shape was changed to the one currently used. The first skateboard exhibition was held in 1963. In 1964, there was a show on TV called "Surf's up" which primarily featured surfers and also some skateboarders. In the same year, a skateboarding magazine called "The Quarterly Skateboard" was launched. It featured popular skateboarders and good models of skateboards. By 1965, skateboards were selling out very quickly and the profits were quite high. Skateboard manufacturers made profits of up to 10 million US dollars.

The shape of the skateboard is small so that it is easier to perform stunts.

The wheels are small and attached to the bottom of the board. They are tightly fixed here.

Skateboarding is a game where people have freely developed many tricks and turns. Even children can perform these tricks.

Though better skateboards were invented in the 1970s, it was not a very popular sport because people did not have a place to practice. Most skateboarding enthusiasts flocked to urban areas. Magazines listed the locations in which skateboarders could come and participate. The skateboarders nicknamed these locations as the "Tea Bowl" or the "Fruit Bowl", owing to the bowl shape of the skateboarding area.

In the later 1970s, the invention of the "ollie" by Alan Ollie Gelfand transformed the world of skateboarding. Ollie essentially remained a unique Florida trick, which was later adapted to the flat ground.

The ollie trick

The ollie trick allowed skateboarders to perform tricks mid-air without the help of any other equipment. Several street skateboarding tricks were evolved from ollie.

In 1995, the International Association of Skateboard Companies was established. The year 2012 saw a new development in skateboarding, the trick of 1080, which was first landed by Tom Schaar.

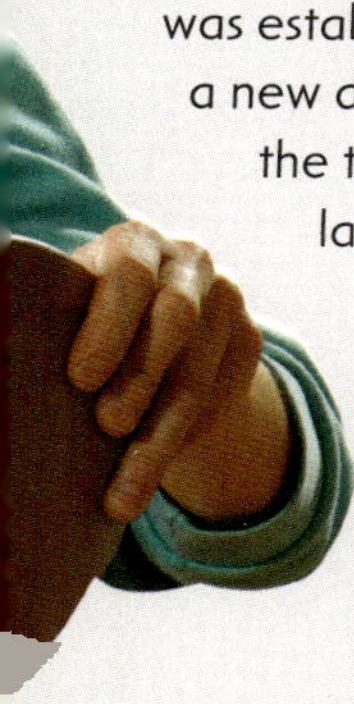

To avoid chances of injury, all the players must wear safety gear like helmets, knee and elbow pads.

Most skaters face injuries on their knees, elbows and wrists because of all the twisting and turning movements involved.

The sport went through significant changes over the years, and its main focus shifted to styles and tricks. It was majorly ruled by two-dimensional freestyling and pivoting stunts. There were also high jumps and long jumps that caught people's attention. Soon enough, kick-flips and 360-degree kick-flips came about. The sport has a high injury risk as it is focussed on balance.

Skateboarding is a sport which people are encouraged to learn at a young age.

Wall of fame

Tony Hawk, Thrasher Magazine's skateboarder of 1990, won the Young Hollywood Culture Icon award in 2002.

Rodney Mullen won the 2002 Trans-World Readers' Choice Award for skater of the year.

Ryan Sheckler, a popular skateboarder, won the 2010 Kids Choice award for Favourite Male Athlete.

One of the interesting trends associated with skateboarding was the sticky sole "slip-on" skate shoes. Skateboarding was actually emulated from the sport of surfing, initially most of the players skateboarded barefoot.

The initially manufactured skateboards lacked traction. Barefoot skateboarders had to deal with foot injuries. This necessitated the need for a special pair of shoes, which had to be specifically designed for the purpose of skateboarding, to allow better traction.

Skateboarders often wear canvas shoes or sports shoes. They should be comfortable in their shoes.

The skateboard causes a lot of friction. Skateboarding barefoot or with the wrong shoes can cause lots of injuries.

Fact card

- By the early 1990s, skateboarding became very popular thanks to TV channels like ESPN and X-Game competitions held by MTV.
- The US military used skateboards to train the armies for sniper fire and tripwire techniques.
- Norway reported so many skateboarding injuries that its government banned the sport for a period of 11 years, from 1978–1989.
- The tricks involved in skateboarding have specific names and styles. An "ollie" is a jump where the front wheels leave the ground first. "Aerials" are stunts which involve floating in the air while using one hand to hold the board.
- Slides involve getting the board up on ledge or rail, or coping and sliding along from there.

Scootering

Scootering is an adventure sport. In this sport, a simple scooter is used to perform daring stunts. Grace and technique are of primary importance in this sport rather than speed or daring.

Riders hold onto the handles and push themselves forward with one foot.

Scooters have a narrow strip where the rider places one or both feet.

Origin

Both scootering and skateboarding developed as adventure sports at around the same time. However, because scooters weigh more than skateboards, cost more and are also inflexible, they did not become as popular as skateboards. By the 1980s, the popularity of this sport decreased a lot. A new wave of scooters was then invented. These scooters were lighter and had smaller wheels.

This modern scooter allowed the rider to perform stunts easily, It also allowed for better control. By 2001, there were many scooters in the game again. The first global scootering competition was held in 2006. San Diego is considered the home of scootering competitions.

Rules

The rules for scoring are very simple. All riders are judged for grace and technique of the move rather than speed. If the rider looks uncomfortable or does not execute the move smoothly, judges can deduct their points.

Types of scootering

Kick scootering can be played on various surfaces. It is treated just like skateboarding. Kick scootering can be performed done in parks, streets and flatlands.

"Indoor scootering" is conducted in arenas. Rails, boxes, vertical ramps, frameworks and other such materials are spread out in the arena to allow the riders to perform their stunts. Indoor scootering parks are sometimes merged with skateboarding parks.

Most riders are involved in freestyle scootering. A lot of skateboarding tricks are incorporated into freestyle scootering.

The bowl-shaped rinks in skate parks are also suitable for scootering.

Fact card

- There is a British magazine called "Scootering" which is a motor scooter magazine.
- In freestyle scootering, riders use kick scooters to perform freestyle tricks.
- In dog scootering, one or more dogs pull a kick scooter forward.

Scooters do not have motors. There is a lot of physical activity involved in moving a scooter. Their tyres are in the shape of mountain bike tyres, but a little smaller. They are called "kick scooters" or "kick bikes" because one needs to kick the ground to push the scooter forward. Dog scooters are not very popular and not many of them are manufactured. Dog scooters have larger tyres that kick scooters. There is also less room for the rider to place his feet. There are no dog scooter competitions.

Sky Surfing

Sky surfing is a mix of board and air sport as it is performed in the sky. The board used is similar to a snowboard. It is strapped to the rider's feet.

Origin

Dominic Jacquet and Jean-Pascal Oron discovered this sport in 1986. Surf Elite was the first company that started the production of sky boards and this contributed to an increase in the popularity of sky surfing. Earlier installments of the boards were not up to the mark as riders faced problems while opening the parachutes.

Later, the boards were improved so that a player could discard it from his/her feet whenever required. Today, skyboarding is considered an extreme adventure sport.

The tricks used in skateboarding also apply here; but, they are performed at much higher altitudes.

Gameplay

Like skateboarding, the rider needs to focus on balancing the body on the board. Even to perform the simplest tricks, the rider needs to have a proper balance on the board. Sky surfing has several acrobatic tricks, which are performed in freefall. The riders let go of the board mid air and dive in different directions. They make quick grabs for the boards or keep a hold on it with one hand. The boards are connected to the diver's shoes.

Riders must wear parachutes for safety reasons. Certain riders wrap ace bandages around their hands and legs in order to maintain their blood circulation in high altitudes. Without these bandages, they would be at a risk when performing high-speed falls during stunts. Spins, rolls, glides and helicopter spins are a few of the most common acrobatic stunts performed. Despite the measures taken, some stunts are too dangerous to be performed by new learners or amateurs, and are best left to professionals.

The popularity of this sport increased when brands like Pepsi and AT&T featured some of the stunts in their commercials.

Skydivers must wear body suits that can endure strong winds.

The skyboard is similar to the skateboard in shape. It does not have wheels at the bottom.

Fact card

- The fundamental sky surfing technique is to stand upright on the board during the freefall, and to tilt the tip of the board down to give it a forward movement.
- Usually, a sky diver is accompanied by another who videotapes the stunts.

Snowboarding

Snowboarding is a fun and adventurous sport. Though there are many snowboarding accidents reported in a year, it is one of the most common sports in snowy regions. In this sport, snowboarders ride down a slope on a snowboard.

Origin

Snowboarding is a very old sport. Back in the 1910s, people slid down the slopes on wooden planks. By 1965, an engineer had developed a crude snowboard. In 1966, the design of snowboards was improved and more than a million snowboards were sold.

Magazines reported snowboarding to be the fastest growing winter sport of the time. The design of the boards kept improving. With every new injury reported, people began to put in tweaks and adjustments that could reduce accidents.

The first national snowboarding race was held in 1982. The first world championship was held in 1985.

Snowboarders should wear goggles to protect their eyes.

All snowboarders wear gloves and warm body suits to maintain their body temperature.

Over the years, snowboarders have come up with several twists and tricks that make the sport more interesting.

The board is flat and curved at the sides to allow easy movement in the snow.

Gameplay

While there are many styles in this sport, only some are allowed in the Olympics. They differ according to the board used.

The most commonly performed tricks are free ride, freestyle and free race. They are mostly similar but have some unique qualities as well.

- **Jibbing:** This focuses mostly on technical riding and performing tricks. This style is a mimic of tricks done in skateboarding and skiing.
- **Free riding:** This is a form of snowboarding which is carried out without any set course. It is based on the challenges of the natural snow slope, and is all about enjoying the experience of snowboarding. Here, a stiffer snowboard is used, which is compact and sturdy. Hence, it helps in maintaining balance and speed.
- **Freestyle:** This is a showboating style, which involves artificial obstacles that allow the rider to perform various stunts. They are also customised into different sizes and lengths. Riders wear soft boots with tipped boards to get better control of the body. All the stunts that are performed on a skateboard are replicated here in the snow.
- **Alpine snowboarding:** This sport takes place on hard-packed snow. It has carving linked turns. It is similar to longboarding or surfing. There is little or no jumping in this style. This type of snowboarding needs extreme balance and weight shifting. It is important to know how to gain speed and to brake on time.
- **Slopestyle:** Competitors are skilled and perform their best tricks while coming down the slope. The slope has several natural and artificial obstacles.

The snowboarder wears warm shoes to keep his/her feet warm. He/she then wears the straps.

This is the strap that allows the snowboarder to fix his/her feet on the board.

The shape of the board is very similar to a skateboard.

Wall of fame

Travis Rice is a snowboarder from the USA. He is placed 13th in the Snowboarder magazine's list of top twenty influential snowboarders in the world. He has won gold medals in the 2003 Aspen games.

Shaun White is a professional snowboarder from the USA. He has won the Olympic gold medal for snowboarding twice. He also holds the X-Games record for winning the most gold medals. He also has the most medals in the competition series. He has won about 10 ESPY awards. He has made several appearances in films and television.

Fact card

- The first modern snowboard was called the "snurfer".
- Snowboarding is an Olympic sport.
- Snowboarding is just like skateboarding without wheels. Even the snowboarding rinks are similar to skateboarding rinks.
- The World Snowboard Federation was founded in 2002.
- "Freeriding" is a type of movement style which appears very fluid to the observer. It involves a lot of jumping and gliding.

Surfboarding

This is the soft board and is mostly used by kids to learn surfing.

Surfboarding is the most widely played sport on the water surface. In this sport, a board is strapped to the surfer's feet. The surfer guides the board over the waves. Surfboarding is classified as an extreme sport.

Origin

The invention of this sport dates back to 1767. It was first observed in Tahiti by Samuel Wallis and his crew, who were the first European visitors to Polynesia. Lieutenant James King was the first person who wrote about the art of surfing.

Mark Twain made a reference to "surfboarding" in one of his works when he wrote that people amused themselves with this sport. George Freeth is known as the father of modern day surfing. He has left behind a legacy of surfboarding.

By 1907, the sport had migrated to California and then spread to other parts of the world. The longboard was introduced to this sport. It made the sport more entertaining for the surfer and the spectator. The concept spread across and by 1975, professional surfing competitions were held regularly in the USA and some parts of Europe.

Surfers move their bodies to adjust to the moving water.

The surfer must keep his hands in check in order to balance himself on the board.

You can see from this point of the water that the surfer is riding the ends of the wave.

The surfers might position themselves on the back, middle or front of the board, depending on the intensity of the wave.

The surfer does not make sudden movements on the board. Otherwise he might lose his balance.

Gameplay

Surfboarding demands accuracy, balance and endurance. Knowledge of swimming is the minimal requirement for this game.

The game has two stages; the beginner and the pro stage. Beginners cut smaller tides and learn to tackle the waves. They use smaller and lighter surfboards, called "soft boards", which are easy to steer. The pro players use larger boards to deal with taller waves.

Surfers are not allowed to have food or alcohol 45 minutes prior to surfing.

The basics of "hold or throw" are to be followed. When the player is paddling, it is better to hold the board. But when the player is about to get wiped out by a wave, it is better to leave the board.

This surfer is riding the very edge of the wave. Surfers do this during the low tide.

In popular surfing areas, parts of the water have red and yellow flags. They indicate the danger spots and warn surfers from going there to surf.

The right-of-way is a rule in which a person closest to the peak of the way has to announce the change in paddling pattern to all other surfers on that wave. Back paddling is avoided.

"Split-peak", that is the surfers going in different directions from the peak, is to be done only when there is no danger to others. If a surfer is riding a wave and another player rides it against him, it is called as a "drop in". This blocks the line and can be extremely dangerous. Hence, dropping in is considered to be the worst thing in surfboarding.

This surfer is riding the interior of the wave. This is mostly done during high tide. It increases the danger and risk involved.

Wall of fame

Kelly Slater is called the "Michael Jordan of the surfing world". He has been an 11 time world champion.

Duke Kahanamoku is a three-time Olympic gold medalist from Hawaii.

Tom Curren is the most stylish surfer. He is a three-time world champion.

Fact card

- Hanging 10 is a popular trick where the surfer stands at the end of the board with his toes curled at the edge of the board.
- The longest surfing ride lasted for 3 hours and 55 minutes and 2 seconds.
- Two or more people can ride on a surfboard together. A world record has been set with 66 people riding on a single surfboard. The board was extremely long and was built just for this purpose.

Wakeboard

This style of wakeboarding is called "cable skiing". Riders are towed along by a cable system instead of a boat.

Wakeboards have foot equipment which keep the wakeboarders fixed to the board.

Wakeboarders must regularly check their boards to make sure they are in shape.

Wakeboarding is a combination of the terms "wake" and "board". Wakeboarders generally use a high-speed boat to tow themselves with the wake.

Origin

Wakeboarding (earlier called "skurfing") developed in the late 1980s after the advent of skiboarding or snowboarding. The sport has many purported origins but it is widely believed that it was created in Australia and New Zealand. Earlier, hand-shaped boards were designed specifically for towing.

In 1983, Howard Jacobs created several wakeboards in the USA by mounting windsurfing foot straps and partial hydroslide pads on some smaller surfboards. He gained popularity by performing backflips on the St. Johns River in Florida. Bruce McKee and his associate Mitchell Ross launched the world's first, mass-produced, plastic, roto-moulded, construction "skurfboard" in Australia.

Rules

There are certain safety regulations that a player has to follow. There are officials or crew members who ensure that all rules are properly checked prior to the game.

A minimum of one safety boat has to be in the vicinity of the wakeboarding zone. There are different classes of the sport—juniors, masters and veterans being the major ones.

Wakeboarders wear gloves to have a stronger grip. Water can loosen the grip.

Wakeboarders wear bodysuits or vests to swim and stay afloat in the water.

Training & Equipment

The various parts of the board that affect its characteristics and handling are:

- Rocker—the bend or curve from tip to tail
- Length—it affects speed and turning capability
- Width—wider boards bounce off the wake harder but turn sluggishly
- Bottom—it directs flow, and decides the lift and drag
- Fins—the placement of fins also affects the release from the wake

Fact card

- Wakeboarders generally travel on water at an average speed of 25–45 kmph. Professionals tend to move faster and travel at an average speed of 60 kmph.